Louisiana

By Judith Jensen Hyde

Subject Consultant
Greg Lambousy
Director of Collections
Louisiana State Museum
New Orleans, Louisiana

Reading Consultant
Cecilia Minden-Cupp, PhD
Former Director of the Language and Literacy Program
Harvard Graduate School of Education
Cambridge, Massachusetts

Children's Press ®
A Division of Scholastic Inc.
New York   Toronto   London   Auckland   Sydney
Mexico City   New Delhi   Hong Kong
Danbury, Connecticut

Designer: Herman Adler
Photo Researcher: Caroline Anderson
The photo on the cover shows a swamp in Louisiana.

Library of Congress Cataloging–in–Publication Data

Hyde, Judith Jensen, 1947–
    Louisiana / by Judith Jensen Hyde.
        p. cm. — (Rookie read–about geography)
    Includes index.
    ISBN 13: 978-0-516-21848-9 (lib. bdg.)   978-0-516-21747-5 (pbk.)
    ISBN 10: 0-516-21848-4 (lib. bdg.)   0-516-21747-X (pbk.)
    1. Louisiana—Juvenile literature. I. Title. II. Series.
    F369.3.H94 2007
    976.3—dc22   2006007154

What has a big mouth, sharp teeth, and lives in Louisiana? An alligator! The alligator is Louisiana's state reptile.

Louisiana is in the southern United States. It touches Texas, Arkansas, Mississippi, and the Gulf of Mexico.

Can you find Louisiana on this map?

A swamp on the West Gulf Coastal Plain

Louisiana is divided into three sections, or regions. These are the East Gulf Coastal Plain, the Mississippi Alluvial (al-LU-vee-uhl) Plain, and the West Gulf Coastal Plain.

The East Gulf Coastal Plain is east of the Mississippi River.

Lousiana black bears and salamanders live in this area.

A salamander

Lake Pontchartrain

The East Gulf Coastal
Plain lies just north
of Lake Pontchartrain
(LAYK PAHNT-shar-trayn).
This is the largest lake
in Louisiana.

The Mississippi Alluvial Plain runs along the Mississippi River from Arkansas to the Gulf of Mexico.

This region is filled with forests, swamps, and lakes.

A swamp on the Mississippi Alluvial Plain

A nutria

The Mississippi Delta
formed where the
Mississippi River meets
the Gulf of Mexico.
A delta is sand and soil
that collect where a river
empties into a larger
body of water.

Swamp rabbits and animals
called nutria (NU-tree-uh)
live in the delta.

The West Gulf Coastal Plain is in western Louisiana.

This region is filled with prairies, hills, and marshes. Marshes are areas of soft, wet, grassy land.

A marsh on the West Gulf Coastal Plain

A Louisiana bayou

Slow-moving streams called bayous (BYE-yooz) flow through marshes in the southern part of the West Gulf Coastal Plain.

Low sandy ridges called cheniers (shuh-NEARS) separate marshes from the gulf.

Baton Rouge (BAHT-uhn RUZH) is the capital of Louisiana and is its largest city.

New Orleans is another famous city in Louisiana. It is famous for its jazz music.

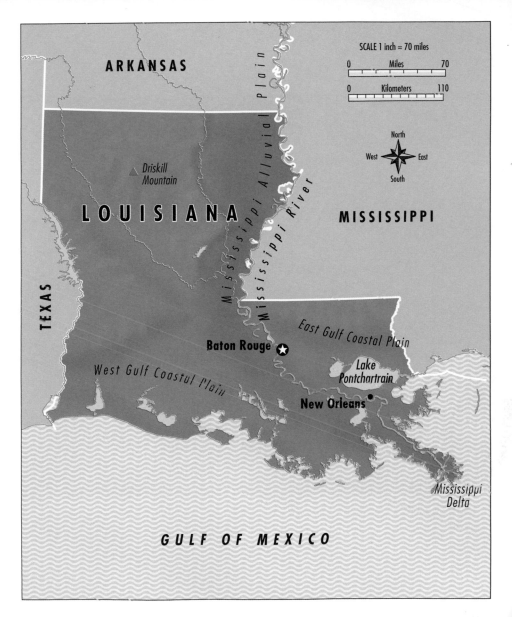

ARKANSAS

SCALE 1 inch = 70 miles

0   Miles   70

0   Kilometers   110

North

West   East

South

Mississippi Alluvial Plain

Driskill
Mountain

LOUISIANA

Mississippi River

MISSISSIPPI

TEXAS

East Gulf Coastal Plain

Baton Rouge ★

Lake
Pontchartrain

West Gulf Coastal Plain

New Orleans •

Mississippi
Delta

GULF OF MEXICO

21

Flooding in New Orleans in 2005

Much of New Orleans
flooded when Hurricane
Katrina hit Louisiana
in 2005. A hurricane
is a storm with strong,
destructive winds.

People in Louisiana are
working hard to rebuild
their state.

Farmers in Louisiana grow cotton and sugarcane plants. The sugar in your home comes from sugarcane.

Louisiana fishers catch shrimp, crabs, and crawfish. Crawfish look like little lobsters.

Other Louisiana products include oil and gas.

A Louisiana fisher catches crawfish.

An eastern brown pelican

Louisiana is home to many animals. Alligators, snakes, and raccoons live here.

Birds often build nests near the water. Louisiana's state bird is the eastern brown pelican.

Maybe one day you'll visit Louisiana!

What will you do first when you get there?

A family canoes through a Louisiana swamp.

Words You Know

alligator

bayou

crawfish

eastern brown pelican

30

Lake Pontchartrain

marsh

nutria

salamander

31

Index

About the Author

For the past several years, Judith Jensen Hyde has worked as a graphic artist and a television technician for a large school district in the Kansas City area. Judith and her husband have one grown daughter, a dog, a cat, and a grand-cat.

Photo Credits

Photographs © 2007: Airphoto-Jim Wark: 10, 31 top left; Corbis Images: cover (Philip Gould), 14, 31 bottom left (George D. Lepp), 9, 31 bottom right (David A. Northcott), 18, 30 top right (Royalty-Free); Dembinsky Photo Assoc.: 6 (Darrell Gulin), 3, 30 top left (Stan Osolinski); John Elk III: 17, 31 top right; Minden Pictures/Tim Fitzharris: 13; NHPA/Mike Lane: 26, 30 bottom right; Photo Researchers, NY: 22 (Wesley Bocxe), 25, 30 bottom left (John Eastcott and Yva Momatiuk); The Image Works/Eastcott-Momatiuk: 29.

Maps by Bob Italiano